American Government

Tribal Governments

by Connor Stratton

www.focusreaders.com

Copyright © 2024 by Focus Readers®, Lake Elmo, MN 55042. All rights reserved. No part of this book may be reproduced or utilized in any form or by any means without written permission from the publisher.

Focus Readers is distributed by North Star Editions:
sales@northstareditions.com | 888-417-0195

Produced for Focus Readers by Red Line Editorial.

Photographs ©: Felicia Fonseca/AP Images, cover, 1; Shutterstock Images, 4, 15; Red Line Editorial, 7; Augustus Robin/Library of Congress, 8; National Photo Company/Library of Congress, 11; 168th Wing Public Affairs/DVIDS, 12; Carlos Osorio/Reuters/Alamy, 17; iStockphoto, 18, 21

Library of Congress Cataloging-in-Publication Data
Names: Stratton, Connor, author.
Title: Tribal governments / by Connor Stratton.
Description: Lake Elmo, MN: Focus Readers, [2024] | Series: American government | Includes bibliographical references and index. | Audience: Grades 2-3
Identifiers: LCCN 2023002951 (print) | LCCN 2023002952 (ebook) | ISBN 9781637395950 (hardcover) | ISBN 9781637396520 (paperback) | ISBN 9781637397657 (pdf) | ISBN 9781637397091 (ebook)
Subjects: LCSH: Indians of North America--Politics and government--Juvenile literature.
Classification: LCC E98.T77 S77 2024 (print) | LCC E98.T77 (ebook) | DDC 321/.1--dc23/eng/20230120
LC record available at https://lccn.loc.gov/2023002951
LC ebook record available at https://lccn.loc.gov/2023002952

Printed in the United States of America
Mankato, MN
082023

About the Author

Connor Stratton writes and edits nonfiction children's books. He lives in Minnesota.

Table of Contents

CHAPTER 1
What They Do 5

CHAPTER 2
History 9

CHAPTER 3
How They Work 13

 A CLOSER LOOK
The Haudenosaunee 16

CHAPTER 4
Tribe, State, Country, Citizen 19

Focus on Tribal Governments • 22
Glossary • 23
To Learn More • 24
Index • 24

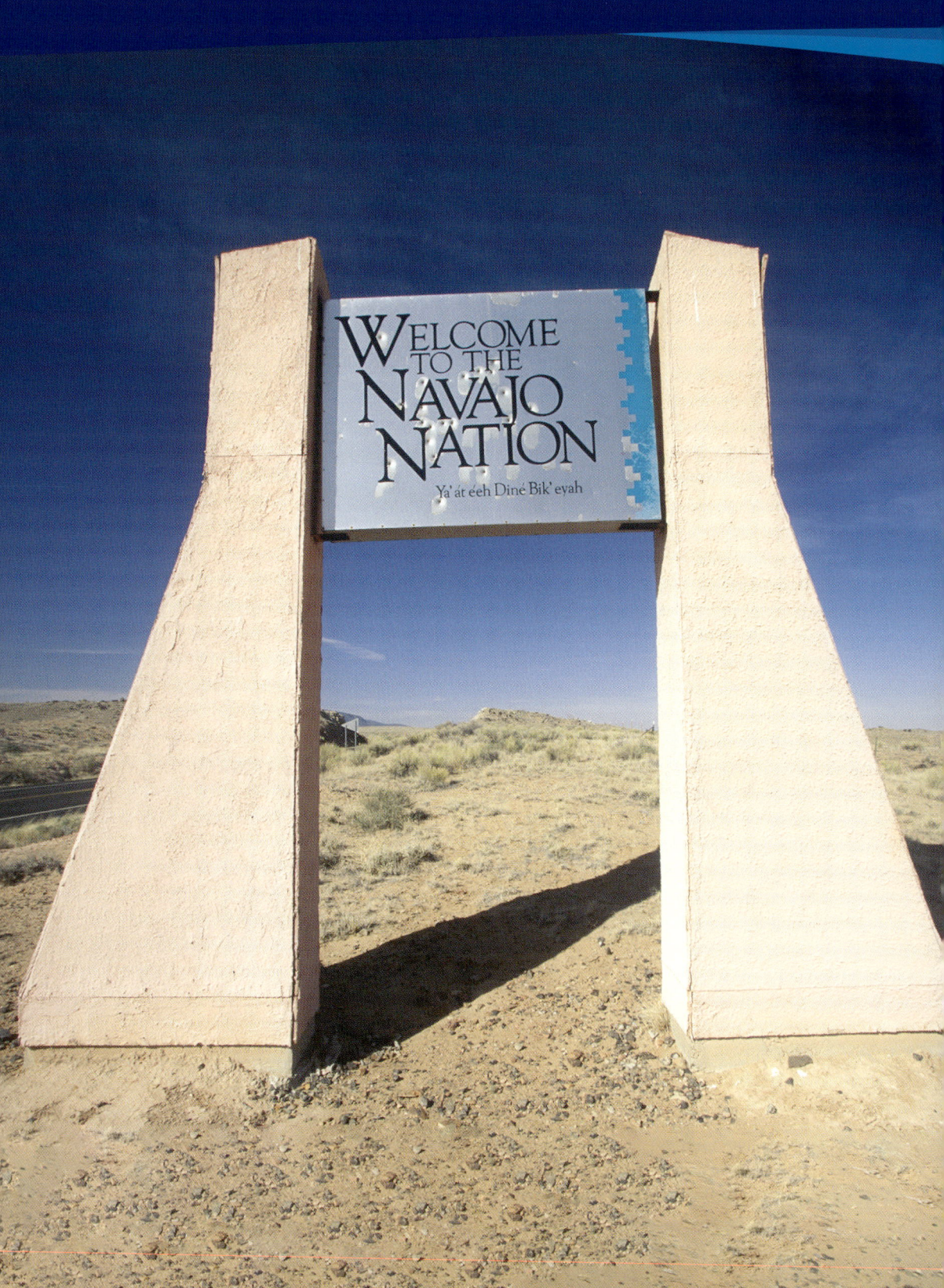

Chapter 1

What They Do

Native nations exist across the United States. They have tribal **governments**. These governments work for their Native **citizens**. They make laws. They make sure people follow those rules.

Tribes offer services, too. Some give health care. Some run schools. Many tribes build roads and buildings. Many also have **reservations**. They control that land. They also take care of it.

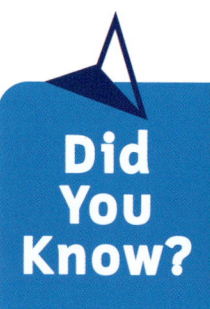 **Did You Know?** Hundreds of tribes are in the United States. More than 200 are in Alaska.

Number of Tribal Governments in the United States

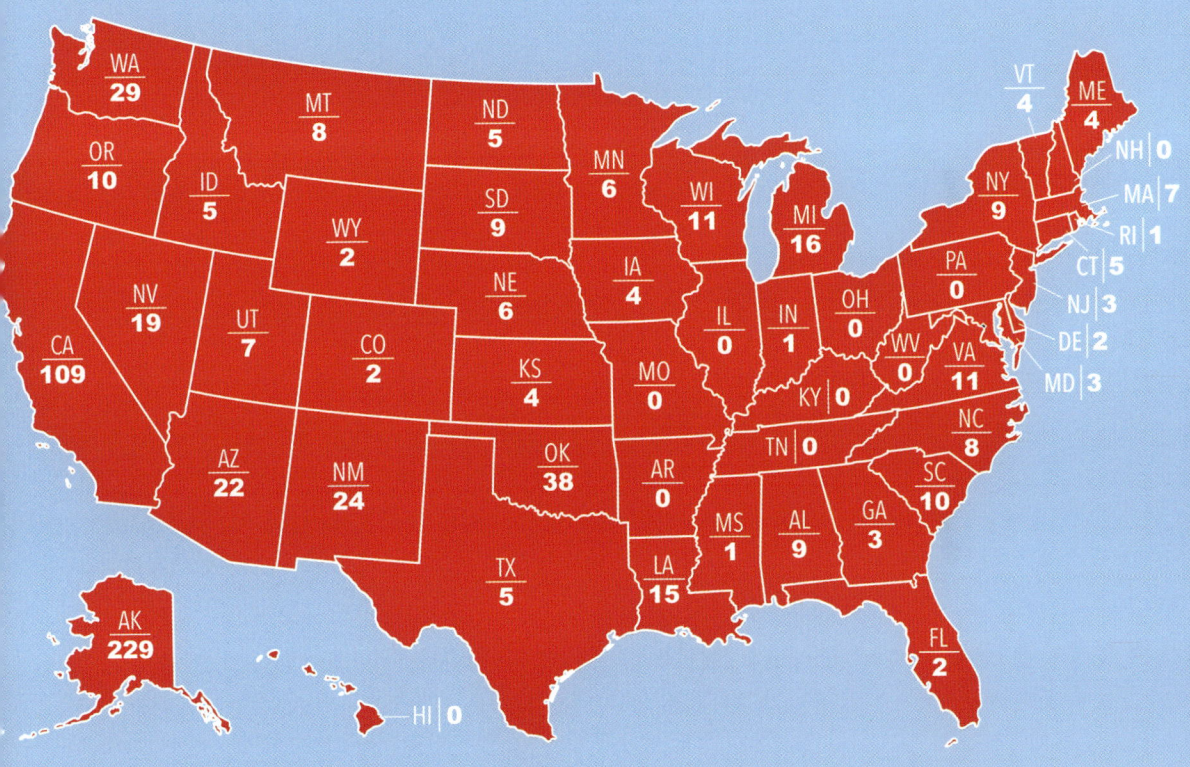

Chapter 2

History

People have lived in America for thousands of years. They formed many nations. People also formed governments. In 1492, a huge change began. European settlers came.

Settlers killed many Native people. They took Native lands. Millions of Native people died. But many Native nations lasted.

The United States formed in 1776. Tribes made **treaties** with the new country.

Did You Know? The United States broke most of the treaties it signed with tribes.

Chapter 3

How They Work

Each tribe is different. Many tribes have **constitutions**. But some do not. Their beliefs and laws are not written down.

Many tribal governments have three parts. These parts are often called branches.

One branch makes laws. Another branch has **judges**. Judges decide questions about laws. The third branch makes sure laws are followed.

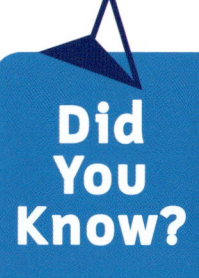 Some governments **represent** more than one Native nation.

A Closer Look

The Haudenosaunee

The Haudenosaunee (*Ho*-de-no-*show*-nee) are a group of six Native nations. Long ago, these nations formed a government. They made a constitution, too. Early US leaders used these ideas in the US Constitution. The Haudenosaunee government is still here today. It is the oldest **democracy** on Earth.

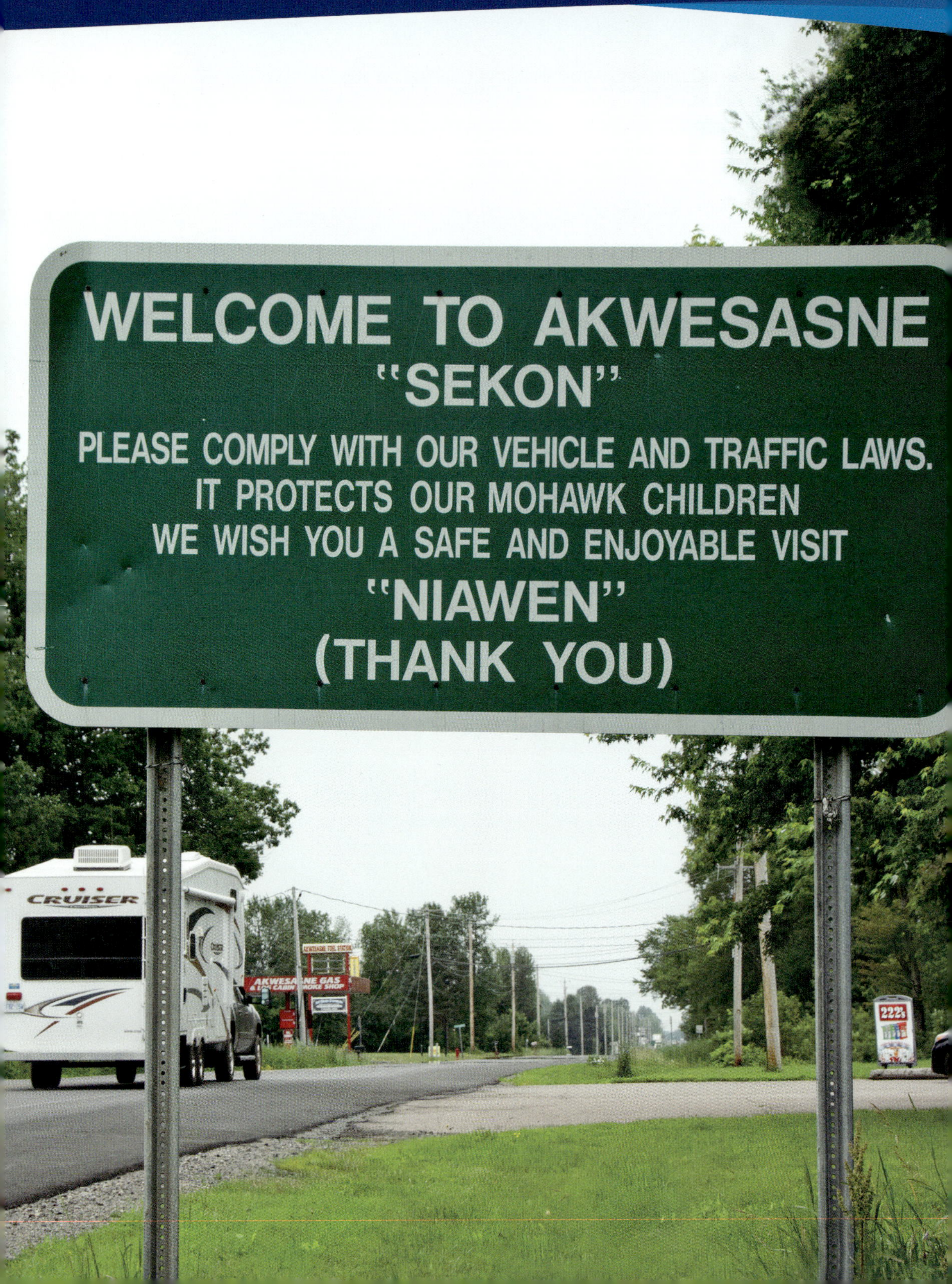
WELCOME TO AKWESASNE
"SEKON"
PLEASE COMPLY WITH OUR VEHICLE AND TRAFFIC LAWS.
IT PROTECTS OUR MOHAWK CHILDREN
WE WISH YOU A SAFE AND ENJOYABLE VISIT
"NIAWEN"
(THANK YOU)

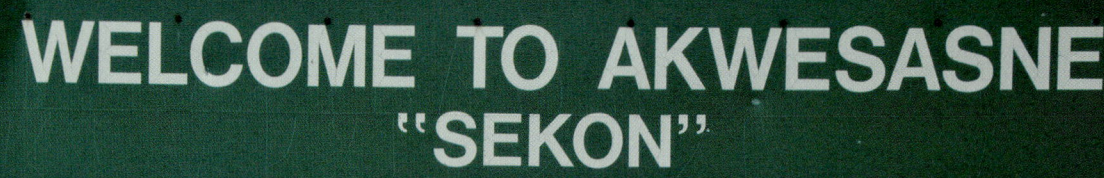

Chapter 4

Tribe, State, Country, Citizen

Tribes are their own nations. They follow many US laws. But the United States must respect tribal laws. Each state must respect tribal laws, too.

Tribes decide who their citizens are. Each tribe has a different way. People often show who they are related to. They show their family was part of the tribe. Then they become citizens.

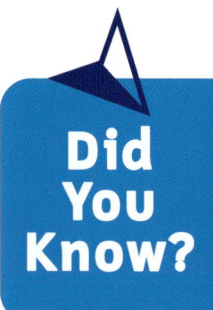

Did You Know? Tribal members are US citizens. They are also citizens of the state they live in.

FOCUS ON
Tribal Governments

Write your answers on a separate piece of paper.

1. Write a few sentences explaining the main ideas of Chapter 2.

2. What was the most interesting thing you learned about tribal governments? Why did you find it interesting?

3. How many tribes are in Alaska?
    - A. fewer than 20
    - B. about 100
    - C. more than 200

4. Tribal members are citizens of which places?
    - A. their tribe only
    - B. their tribe and their state
    - C. their tribe, their state, and the United States

Answer key on page 24.

Glossary

citizens
People who are members of a country, state, or tribe and have rights as a result.

constitutions
Documents laying out the basic beliefs and laws of tribes, states, or countries.

democracy
A system of government in which the people have power. Democracies often have elections.

governments
The people and groups that run cities, states, tribes, or countries.

judges
People who decide cases in courts of law.

represent
To speak and act on behalf of a person or group.

reservations
Areas of land set aside for Native peoples.

treaties
Official agreements that are made between two or more countries or groups.

To Learn More

BOOKS

Lajiness, Katie. *Mohawk*. Minneapolis: Abdo Publishing, 2019.

Sorell, Traci. *We Are Still Here!: Native American Truths Everyone Should Know*. Watertown, MA: Charlesbridge Publishing, 2021.

NOTE TO EDUCATORS

Visit **www.focusreaders.com** to find lesson plans, activities, links, and other resources related to this title.

Index

C
constitutions, 13, 16

H
Haudenosaunee, 16

R
reservations, 6

T
treaties, 10

Answer Key: 1. Answers will vary; 2. Answers will vary; 3. C; 4. C